I am the Lorax. I speak for the trees.

—from *The Lorax*

The editors would like to thank
ROBERT D. FRIEDEL, PhD,
Professor Emeritus, University of Maryland, Department of History,
for his assistance in the preparation of this book.

All photographs used under license from Shutterstock.com, with the following exceptions:
Photographs courtesy Waterfront Partnership of Baltimore, front cover, pp. 8–9; Boeri Studio/Dimitar
Harizanov (graphic processing by Penguin Random House), pp. 10–11; Ooho/David Lineton, p. 12
(bottom photograph); The FRESHGLOW Co., pp. 14–15 (bottom four photographs of FreshPaper
sheets), p. 15 (top photograph); Folia Water, pp. 16–17; Reeddi, p. 19; Living Seawalls/Alex Goad,
pp. 24–25; CAKE, p. 29 (bottom two photographs), bottom back cover.

Visit us on the Web!
Seussville.com
rhcbooks.com

Educators and librarians, for a variety of teaching tools, visit us at RHTeachersLibrarians.com

Library of Congress Cataloging-in-Publication Data is available upon request.
ISBN 978-0-593-48804-1 (trade) — ISBN 978-0-593-48805-8 (lib. bdg.)

MANUFACTURED IN CHINA

10 9 8 7 6 5 4 3 2 1

First Edition

Green Machines

and Other Amazing Eco-Inventions

by Michelle Meadows

illustrated by Aristides Ruiz

Random House 🏠 New York

I am the Lorax,
and we're here to celebrate
eco-friendly inventions
that people create.

What makes them eco-friendly?
Here is what I mean—
it's the way these inventions
keep our planet green.

LOVE the EARTH

OUR PLANET OUR HOME

CLEAN EARTH GREEN EARTH

PROTECT OUR PLANET

OUR EARTH, OUR RESPONSIBILITY

GO GREEN!

PROTECT the EARTH

GO GREEN!

GREEN MACHINES

SAVE the PLA

They help clean our water.

They help save energy.

They fight air pollution.

Turn the page and see!

Mr. Trash Wheel

When rivers and streams
fill with garbage and litter,
it pollutes the water
and harms every critter.

Enter Mr. Trash Wheel!

He gobbles up garbage
that flows into his mouth
on a Baltimore river
as it flows north to south.

The water and sun
make his giant wheel spin,
moving trash forward
till it drops in his bin.

Vertical Forests

All over the world,
in cities everywhere,
fossil fuel fumes
are polluting the air.

So designers created
a clever solution—
planting forests ON buildings
to fight air pollution!

On these green balconies
birds and bugs have it made.
The plants clean the air
and provide lots of shade.

Ooho

Plastic bottles cause trouble,
I'm sure you'll agree.
They fill up our landfills
and pollute the sea.

This Ooho is a small thing
that does a BIG job.
It's a bottle you eat—
yes, an edible blob!

Just take a small nibble
to make the blob burst.
Then out flows fresh water
to satisfy your thirst.

Made of seaweed and plants,
these blobs have no taste.
Hooray for new products
that don't create waste!

FreshPaper

Each year lots of fruit
and veggies go to waste.
Sometimes food can spoil
before people get a taste.

FreshPaper slows produce
from rotting away.
Spices inside the paper
help prevent decay.

Put a sheet in a bowl,
a container, or bag,
or into a fridge drawer
and your lettuce won't sag!

Up to four times as long,
your produce stays edible.
Cutting food waste with spice?
That's simply incredible!

Folia Filters

Drinking dirty water
causes illness and disease.
But these simple paper filters
remove dirt and germs with ease.

The secret's in the paper.
There is silver inside.
It kills germs in the water.
Dirt has nowhere to hide!

LID

Place a filter in a funnel
that's shaped like a cone.

Then attach a water bottle
just as I've shown.

Flip the whole thing over.
Glug, glug, glug, glug. Glug.
Safe drinking water
flows into a clean jug!

Reeddi ("Ready") Capsule

We rely on electricity
at our jobs and in our homes
to power our appliances,
our computers, and our phones.

And when the power goes out?

Well, it isn't ANY fun.

Our devices all go silent.

Our work does not get done.

Behold the Reeddi battery!
It draws power from the sun,
storing electricity
to make devices run.

A Reeddi battery is rented
from a solar-charged machine.
Affordable clean energy
is a SMART way to go green!

Planting Trees Using Drones

Trees produce oxygen.

They help clean the air.

They keep the planet cool.

They reduce sunlight and glare.

But we lose billions
of Earth's trees every year.
It's called deforestation
when whole forests disappear.

They're cut down for many reasons
and sometimes destroyed by fire.
But WHATEVER the reason,
the impact it has is dire.

To plant new trees by hand
is expensive, hard, and slow.
But there IS a faster way I know
to make a forest grow!

This drone is an aircraft
that travels way up high.
No pilot is needed
to fly through the sky.

Drones fire seed pods
down into the ground.
In hard-to-reach spaces,
they spread seeds around.

Not every seed will sprout,

but many will with time.

They'll grow into fine trees.

Which one would YOU climb?

Did you know?
Drones can plant thousands of seeds
a day.

Living Seawalls

Seawalls are flat structures
that protect the shore.
But LIVING seawalls protect
the shore and much more!

Made of tiles shaped like
things found in the sea.
Nooks and crannies create
shelter naturally.

Bolted onto seawalls,
the tiles become home
to many plants and animals
and a place for fish to roam.

Did you know?
Seawalls protect the shore from erosion.
Most have smooth surfaces that are
hard for marine life to latch onto.

Protecting Wildlife with Electric Bush Bikes

Poachers hunt illegally.

They shouldn't, but they do.

They hurt endangered animals.

I'm sorry, but it's true.

Rangers try to catch them
as poachers hunt their prey.
But when poachers hear them coming,
they often get away.

To try to solve this problem
and keep wildlife from dangers,
the maker of a motorbike
joined forces with the rangers.

Together they designed
an electric motorbike
with a very special feature
that poachers do NOT like.

POACH
COACH

This electric bike is quiet,

a feature that is wise.

Rangers can get close to poachers

and catch them by surprise!

POACH COACH

Powered by the sun,

solar bush bikes don't use fuel.

Saving wildlife on motorbikes?

This green machine is COOL!

Did you know?

Rangers are trained to keep the world's most endangered species safe.

When inventors see a problem,
they ask, "What can we do?"
Then they work to find solutions
or create something new.

They ask a LOT of questions:
What? How? Why? and Who?
They design and test new products
and new ways to do things, too.

Some inventors work alone
and others as a team.
They try and try and try again.
They keep following their dream!

Some are young and some are old,

and some are in-between.

Some are scientists and some are not.

But one thing I have seen . . .

. . . inventors study the inventions
of those who came before,
then work to make improvements
to make a thing do MORE!

HEDY LAMARR

WIRELESS
FIDELITY

THOMAS ALVA EDISON
ELECTRICITY

GEORGE WASHINGTON CARVER
AGRICULTURE

Think like an inventor.
Imagine what COULD be.
Making the world better
takes creativity.

Explore possibilities.
Check facts and compare.
Try to think outside the box
to solve problems with flair.

CREATIVE JUICE

Keep an open mind.

Let creative juices flow.

And remember that a small idea

can grow and grow and grow!

Big
Idea

Brainstorm Your OWN Invention!

A brainstorm isn't a weather event—it's a way to come up with ideas! Brainstorming is easy and fun, and you can do it alone or in a group. Just remember, there are no BAD ideas. And the more ideas the better!

You will need:

- lined paper
- drawing paper
- a pencil or pen
- your imagination
- markers or crayons
- poster paper (optional)

1. Write a list of all the problems you would like to solve.

2. Choose one problem to focus on.

3. Use your imagination to create an invention to solve the problem.

4. Ask yourself these questions, and write down your answers:

- What do I need my invention to do?
- How would my invention solve the problem?
- What are the benefits of my invention?
- Would it help people or the environment?
- Would it save money or time?
- Who would benefit from using my invention?
- How does my invention work?
- What does my invention look like?

5. Sketch your invention. Once you are happy with your drawing, label its parts and use markers or crayons to add color.

6. If you'd like, copy your drawing onto poster paper and use it to pitch your idea to your family or classroom. Explain how your new invention solves a problem, and see if anyone has suggestions for improving it. Remember, inventors are always looking for ways to improve their inventions!

About the Inventions and Inventors

Mr. Trash Wheel

Environmental scientist and shipbuilder **John Kellett** was inspired to invent Mr. Trash Wheel during his morning walk to work. As he crossed a footbridge over the Jones Falls River, he saw what looked like a conveyor belt of trash flowing into Baltimore's Inner Harbor. He contacted the city of Baltimore to see if they were open to ideas on how to solve the problem, and he began sketching! Kellett's friend and community planner **Adam Lindquist** added googly eyes and named the invention Mr. Trash Wheel to help engage the community. Today, a whole *family* of Trash Wheels keeps the Inner Harbor clean! To learn about them all, visit mrtrashwheel.com.

Vertical Forests

Architect **Stefano Boeri** created the Vertical Forest, a high-rise residential building full of greenery on balconies that combats air pollution. Consisting of hundreds of trees and thousands of shrubs and plants, his buildings absorb dust in the air and reduce pollution in the city. Vertical Forests are planted in cities around the world. Check out stefanoboeriarchitetti.net/en /vertical-foresting for more information, and search online for videos of the amazing flying gardeners who care for these forests!

Ooho

Ooho is an alternative to plastic bottles for on-the-go consumption. It is a type of sustainable packaging made of seaweed and plants. Architect and designer **Rodrigo García González** and **Pierre-Yves Paslier** invented this edible packaging to reduce plastic waste. The company González and Paslier founded (called Notpla for "Not Plastic") is developing new ways to use the material they invented for other sustainable packaging, like ketchup packets and take-out food cartons that do not include plastic. Visit notpla.com for more information.

FreshPaper

Kavita Shukla, founder and CEO of the FRESHGLOW Co., invented FreshPaper to address the problem of food waste. The invention started as a middle school science project and was inspired by her grandmother's herbal mixture from India. Shukla began conducting experiments with an Indian herb called fenugreek and found that it can preserve food and slow bacterial growth. For more information, visit freshglow.co.

Folia Filters

Theresa Dankovich invented these germ-killing water filters when she was a graduate student studying chemistry. She wanted to create an affordable water purifier for people in the world who need it the most. Dankovich's team has field-tested her inexpensive filters in South Africa, Ghana, Honduras, Kenya, and Haiti, and they are currently being sold in Bangladesh. For more information, visit foliawater.com.

Reeddi Capsule

Olugbenga Olubanjo, CEO of Reeddi, invented this solar-powered battery to charge up devices and provide power in locations without electricity. Reeddi energy stations are powered with solar panels, and customers pay a small fee to rent a Reeddi capsule. The capsule can power lights, mobile phones, laptops, televisions, and other devices. The company plans to expand across Nigeria and launch in other parts of Africa and Southeast Asia. Vist reeddi.com for more information.

Planting Trees Using Drones

To address the problem of deforestation and fight climate change, multiple companies around the world use drones to plant new trees. Computer software helps identify the best places to plant, and the drones fire seed pods into the ground with precision. Drones are also useful for planting seeds in places that are difficult for people to reach.

Living Seawalls

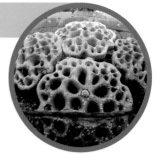

Living Seawalls were created by marine ecologists at the Sydney Institute of Marine Science, Macquarie University, and University of New South Wales in Australia—**Dr. Melanie Bishop, Dr. Katherine Dafforn,** and **Dr. Mariana Mayer Pinto**— and industrial designer **Alex Goad** at Reef Design Lab. Living Seawalls return natural habitat features to artificial flat seawalls to provide protection and homes for a wide variety of animals and seaweeds. For more information, visit livingseawalls.com.au.

Protecting Wildlife with Electric Bush Bikes

Swedish motorbike company **CAKE** collaborated with the **Southern African Wildlife College** in South Africa to design motorbikes to help save endangered species from poaching. Instead of using noisy motorcycles powered by gasoline, now rangers can use solar-powered bikes that don't make a lot of noise. For more information, visit ridecake.com/en-US/anti-poaching.

43

Glossary

Deforestation: The removal of a large area of trees.

Dire: A serious or urgent situation.

Drone: An aircraft without a pilot that's operated by remote control.

Eco-friendly inventions: Inventions that help the environment.

Electricity: The flow of electrical power or charge.

Energy: The ability to do work.

Environment: The surroundings in which people, animals, and plants live.

Fossil fuel: Coal, oil, and natural gas.

Oxygen: Colorless gas that exists in the air.

Poaching: The illegal practice of trespassing to hunt wildlife, which reduces the population of animals.

Pollution: The presence in the environment of a harmful or poisonous substance.

Produce: Fruits and vegetables.

Solar energy: Heat and light energy produced by the sun.

Index

The LORAX
Dr. Seuss

Encourage a love of nature
and respect for the environment in children of ALL ages
with these books featuring Dr. Seuss's Lorax!